LES,
Best wishes
Love
Margaret, Brian
fiona and marcia

High Wycombe

in old picture postcards

by
Ivan G. Sparkes

European Library - Zaltbommel/Netherlands MCMLXXXIII

GB   ISBN 90 288 2576 2

European Library in Zaltbommel/Netherlands publishes among other things the following series:

IN OLD PICTURE POSTCARDS *is a series of books which sets out to show what a particular place looked like and what life was like in Victorian and Edwardian times. A book about virtually every town in the United Kingdom is to be published in this series. By the end of this year about 75 different volumes will have appeared. 1,250 books have already been published devoted to the Netherlands with the title* **In oude ansichten.** *In Germany, Austria and Switzerland 500, 60 and 15 books have been published as* **In alten Ansichten;** *in France by the name* **En cartes postales anciennes** *and in Belgium as* **En cartes postales anciennes** *and/or* **In oude prentkaarten** *150 respectively 400 volumes have been published.*

For further particulars about published or forthcoming books, apply to your bookseller or direct to the publisher.

This edition has been printed and bound by Grafisch Bedrijf De Steigerpoort in Zaltbommel/Netherlands.

INTRODUCTION

To most of the world, High Wycombe is the Furniture Centre of Great Britain, and possibly of Europe itself, but to the residents of the town, whose families have lived here for many generations, High Wycombe is a place which has changed rapidly over the past twenty-five years from a closely knit community, with a crowded but attractive town centre, to a fragmented society cut in two by a modern shopping centre and large areas of waste-land created from the sites of demolished nineteenth century houses.

The chair industry was not the first major industry of High Wycombe, as the many water mills on the River Wye had been utilised for grinding grain for flour, for fulling cloth for its textile industry, and for pulping rags for its paper industry over a period of seven hundred years before the first Windsor Chair emerged. It is true however, that the town's expertise in promoting and exploiting commercial opportunites found its 'finest hour' when the beechwoods which grew in profusion around the Chilterns, fell victim to the latest craft. An industry which was existing in the 1730's as a cottage craft built up in the next three or four decades to adopt mass production methods which culminated in the 1860's with an estimated 5,000 chairs a day being produced in the area. The Bodger or chair-leg turner in the woods, was at the beginning of the process, making the chair-legs, stretchers and sticks which were brought into the factories of High Wycombe to be made into the Windsor chairs for which the area is famous.

In time the industry changed its emphasis and furniture of different types came from its production lines, and although at times the town was noted for its 'cheap chairs', over the years many fine craftsmen have made fine furniture for churches, cathedrals, guilds and royalty.

The Borough, although involved deeply in the industries of the time progressed over the years creating its own burgesses, appointed aldermen and Mayors and electing its Members of Parliament from the thirteenth century. The town was responsible for its own fairs and affairs from the twelfth century, and out of this grew the independance of mind which became a feature of the Borough's approach to most matters affecting its welfare.

The original boundaries were very small, they extended from Frogmore to Pann Mill, and from the Railway Station to the Wycombe Abbey; but gradually over the late nineteenth century up to the 1930's they were pushed further and further into the surrounding countryside. Following the Second World War, the industrial scene changed, with more types of industry filling the several industrial estates established in the Borough. Eventually in April 1974, following the Local Government Re-organisation Act, the Borough merged with Wycombe Rural District Council and Marlow Urban District Council into the new Wycombe District Council. The administrative centre is still in High Wycombe, but the new District covers an area many times larger than the earlier authority. The several traditions of the old Borough of Chepping Wycombe are still carried on in the hands of the new 'Charter Trustees' who are those Councillors in the District Council representing the Wards of the former Borough.

1. This view across High Wycombe from Keep Hill in the 1920's gives a good impression of the wooded nature of the town centre and the surrounding hills at that time. Although much building has taken place, especially on the northern hills overlooking the Wye valley, much open countryside still remains.

2. Marlow Hill was the southern approach to the town and the visitor travelled between the lodge-gates of Wycombe Abbey, which stood on each side of the Marlow Road. The gates on the left still remain, but in the past forty years, the hill has been widened and straightened to make it a double carriage-way which now leads on to the multi-roundabout in front of the Abbey.

3. Facing over the valley was the Memorial Hospital, opened in 1923, built as a memorial to the fallen in the First World War. This replaced the former Cottage Hospital in Priory Road. This building was in its turn demolished to make way for the new Wycombe General Hospital, which was built in the 1960's.

Wycombe Abbey

High Wycombe

4. Wycombe Abbey stands on the site of the old Manor House of Loakes, an estate which passed to Henry Petty, in 1700, and was disposed of, by the Marquess of Lansdowne in 1798. The present building was enlarged and re-modelled in 1795 to plans of James Wyatt. It was purchased by the Girls' Education Company Ltd. and opened in 1896 as the famous Wycombe Abbey School. During the Second World War Wycombe Abbey was the Headquarters of the U.S. 8th Army Air Force, and during one of his tours of Britain, Glen Miller played at the Abbey.

5. The Carrington Family, who owned the Abbey in the nineteenth century, had strong connections with Bucks Military life, and it was the centre of army activity in High Wycombe in the First World War. Here we see a fine collection of vintage cars lined up ready to move off, about 1914.

6. The Wycombe Excelsior Cyclists Club was formed in 1882 in High Wycombe, to which both bi-cyclists and tri-cyclists were admitted. Here a group of cyclists on most unusual cycles posed in the grounds of Wycombe Abbey.

7. The grounds of Wycombe Abbey adjoined the Rye, which was an open space adjacent to Pan Mill and the Hospital of St. John and following the death of Viscount Wendover, Lord Carrington's son, in the First World War, this stretch of path with its trees was given to the public in his memory and called Wendover Way.

8. An the end of Wendover Way and the Dyke was the Cascade and the Grotto, which formed a pretty picture in 1910 when this picture was taken. Unfortunately time has overtaken it, the grotto is blocked up, and the cascade has less majesty than in the past.

9. When the Abbey was sold to become the Girls' School, the entrance drive was laid out as Queen Victoria Road, with the first building 'The Town Hall', opened in 1904 to designs of J.J. Bateman and C.E. & A. Hale. In time the civic buildings increased, with the Library, shown attached to the Town Hall, opened in 1932.

10. The tranquility of Queen Victoria Gardens is very evident in this view of the River Wye passing under the bridge next to the Police Station. To the right are the Municipal Offices, opened 1932, and in the distance the Liberal Club, which moved from High Street about the same time. The Post Office moved into Queen Victoria Road in 1934 from Easton Street, and the Police Station from Newlands in 1935.

11. This coach outing, waiting to set off, stands against the rich foliage of the trees which stood on the site of the Police Station. The ladies are possible off to Burnham Beeches, which was frequently the venue for trips out into the country.

12. Queen Victoria Road opened into Easton Street on the right, which takes its name from East Town, as it was was the east side of the High Street. The large house in the foreground was always the Doctor's house, and Dr. S.P. Huggins was probably the last to practice there before that house, and the shop of A. Dean, clothier, were demolished in the widening of Crendon Street.

13. Moving down Easton Street towards the Rye was 'The Greyhound' public house, and looking back towards the Guildhall can be seen the turrets of the Rupert Gates which fronted the carriageway to Wycombe Abbey.

13TH. CENTURY RUINS, HIGH WYCOMBE.

14. These are the ruins of St. John's Hospital, one of the oldest buildings in High Wycombe other than the parish church. It stands at the east end of Easton Street, opposite the new Law Courts, and was a form of mediaeval hostel with a chapel attached. It was built thirteenth century and had its own annual fair, and until the Reformation, St. Johns' was an important part of the religious life of High Wycombe. In 1562 Queen Elizabeth granted a Royal charter to create the Royal Grammar School in its place.

15. As the town grew, so did the Royal Grammar School, until it outgrew the old mediaeval building, and in 1883 this typical Victorian building in red and yellow brick was built to replace it. It was only due to the persistence of the Society of Antiquaries of London, and of similar organisations outside the town, that the remains of the thirteenth century building were retained, and the Hospital not demolished entirely.

16. Another new Royal Grammar School was needed in Edwardian times, and once more rebuilt, this time to designs of Arthur Vernon, and moved to open land at the top of Amersham Hill. The new building was opened in 1915, and more recently, the extensions in front of the building were opened by Queen Elizabeth II in 1962 during the celebrations of the 400th anniversary of the school's charter.

17. Passing the Hospital of St. John the visitor came to the 'Coach and Horses' public
house which had an archway which led behind into a small group of streets with little
terraced houses, a world almost on its own. All this was demolished in the 1960's and the
open car-park, next the Trinity Chapel, stands in its stead.

18. Pann Mill and Trinity Church have been the subject of many postcards, and the mill pond, reflecting the two towers of the Congregational Church, make a most attractive picture. The mills on the Wye river go back to Norman times, and they played an active part in the growth of the industrial life of the town. Pann Mill has gone, demolished in 1972, but the mill-wheel has been preserved. It is to be renovated and will be turning again in the near future, as it forms part of a project of the High Wycombe Society.

19. London Road in 1910 shows the width of the River Wye at that time, as it flowed swiftly from its source near West Wycombe, down through the Wye Valley into the River Thames. Much of its width has been infilled to make the gardens bordering its banks, and the rough grass shown in the postcards has been replaced by paths, a children's play area and mown grass.

HIGH WYCOMBE.

20. The old Hayward's Cottage was on the edge of the River Wye and with access to the Ryemead, for his job was the ensure that the cattle allowed on the common belonging to the burgesses of Chepping Wycombe were looked after, and herded off at the correct time each evening. Each burgess had the right to have two cows and a heifer grazing on the Rye, and the Hayward, who was appointed by the Corporation, earned £2 a year in 1876, he was also given livery, the house, and fees from cattle pasturage.

21. Marsh Green follows the Rye and Holymead as you follow the course of the River Wye, and in this postcard can be seen the buildings of Bassetsbury on the right with the Bassetsbury Barn in the forefront. This was the area for the watercressbeds, and the flooded area to the left of the picture has since been drained, and the Express Dairy now stands roughly where the buildings on the left appear.

Darvill Mill, High Wycombe.

22. Darvill Mill was next along the path, generally known as Marsh Green Mill; this was a paper mill, for papermaking was an important industry in the Wye Valley from the seventeenth century through into the twentieth century. Records show that this mill was in the possession of Hugh Stratton, paper maker in 1750, and that he was succeeded by William Veary, who was still making paper in 1816.

23. The river carries on along Back Lane, and this footbridge crossing its width is probably the one near the 'King George V' public house. It had earlier been named the 'King of Prussia', but the wave of ill feeling against the Germans at the outset of the First World War, caused this name to be changed to the then reigning English monarch.

51395.

24. Wycombe Marsh was well out of the actual borough, but it still has strong links with the town, being as it was, within the Parish of Chepping Wycombe, and in the 'foreigns'. This view is just alongside the Church of St. Anne and the Baptist Church next to Davenport Vernon's garage.

25. Back along the lane to Keep Hill and to the approaches of the Rye. The swans on the water are a good reminder of the arms of the Borough, which go back to the sixteenth century, and include the symbol of the swan with closed wings and a golden chain around it and a ducal coronet around its neck. This was the badge of the de Bohun Family, which in mediaeval times owned much land in this area.

26. High Street in the 1840's, taken from an oil painting by E.J. Niemann. This gives an impression of spaciousness we seem to have lost with the introduction of pavements, bollards, street lamps and vehicles. The trees on the left, halfway down the High Street, were in the garden of 'Navarino House' and the Halifax Building Society premises of red brick were built here in the late nineteenth century.

27. Navarino House was an elegant town house type building on the site of the present W.H. Smith & Son site, and it replace the earlier 'Katherine Wheel' public house, which has been destroyed by fire. It was to this inn that King Charles and his retinue came, and stayed overnight during a visit to the town in November 1663. At one time the house was the lace depository of Daniel Hearn, who is reputed to have built it circa 1837. The House was later called 'Buckingham House', but locally was more familiarly known as 'Bobbin House', because of its connections with the lace industry in the town.

28. The Rupert Gates, now rebuilt half-way up Marlow Hill, were the entrance gates to Wycombe Abbey, and they stood in front of what is now the Museum Gardens which adjoin the Library. The carriageway led down what is now Queen Victoria Road, across the bridge, still bearing the plate announcing it as built in memory of Queen Victoria, to the Abbey itself. These gates were removed stone by stone when the Girls's School purchased the Abbey, and moved to become the entrance gates of Daws Hill House, to which Lord Carrington moved after leaving the Abbey.

29. High Street, about 1905, still had an elegance about it, the Guildhall sat firmly at the end of the street surveyed the whole area of Church Square and Cornmarket, the lamp in the middle of the street is very delicate, and it lights both High Street and the new street, built in 1900, called Corporation Street on which Lloyd's Bank stands on the corner.

30. Just adjacent to Lloyd's Bank is the jewellers shop of C.H. Berry Ltd., which was in the eighteenth and early nineteenth century the site of the 'Unicorn Inn'. This building had for some time been connected with the military in the town, and in 1799 it was converted into the Wycombe Military College. In time a junior department was opened in Marlow and in 1813 that moved to Sandhurst, while the senior branch at High Wycombe moved to Farnham in Surrey.

31. Opposite Lloyd's Bank in Corporation Street was the vast emporium of Davenport and Vernon, where they sold all forms of ironmongery, household goods, and even, as they came, cars and bicycles and it became the centre for the local motor-cycling club. On the right of the picture is the back of the open-top-horse-bus which journeyed from West Wycombe to Loudwater, stopping at High Wycombe, and charging one penny for each section of the route.

32. The Davenport Brothers are reputed to be shown here, exhibiting the latest types of bicycle available from Davenport Vernon's stores on the corner of Corporation Street, now Fad's the decorating shop.

33. Probably the most popular and well-known hostelry in the town was the 'Red Lion', shown here as the Hunt gathers ready to be off for a day's hunting. It also seems that an election is in the offing, as a poster declares the name of 'Browning' as a possible candidate. The archway to the right of the portico led to the stables, and in the days of the coaching, this was a place for changing horses and having a meal on the journey to or from London. Next door is the Liberal Club, which in time moved to its present premises next to the Fire Station.

34. High Street has always been the scene of special events, and here the band, followed by carnival floats including a group of children in white surrounding a maypole are travelling along towards the entrance gates of Wycombe Abbey. The ladies looking over the balcony to the right are standing at what is now the window of Abbey National, while the sign of 'Central Hall' marks the present opening of Corporation Street.

35. As the parade continued, along came a cart loaded up with chairs. This was the normal method of taking the newly made chairs across the countryside, but here, the cart is loaded up with six hundred chairs, almost twice the normal load. Behind rides the Lifeboat crew, for this is known as the Lifeboat Parade, the benefits of which would probably go to that organisation.

36. The Lifeboat itself followed, and after a long haul through the town would have been launched on the Dyke. This always caused great hilarity, as the Mayor and selected members of the Corporation joined the crew in a trip from end to end of this length of water. The parade is later than those in the period postcards, as the Lloyd's Bank and the entrance to Corporation Street have been built.

37. Even wilder scenes were observed in the streets of High Wycombe following the news of the Relief of Mafeking on 18th May 1900. This British unit had been relieved after a seven month siege by the Boers in South Africa, and throughout the country wild scenes of excitement were experienced. At the end of the War, the local troops came back to a heroes welcome with archways at the Station, in High Street and in St. Mary Street.

38. The popularity of Queen Victoria was at its height at the time of her Golden Jubilee in 1887 and her Diamond Jubilee in 1897. On each occasion great preparations were made for celebrations in the town. This postcard shows the school children all lined up in their classes ready to enter the Wycombe Abbey for a tea and games. But first they had to sing the Doxology followed by the National Anthem and just before four o'clock the signal was given for the singing of grace. 'Great urns of tea were quickly emptied and plates of bread and butter and cakes were cleared with magical rapidity.'

39. Following the Jubilee tea the cry was 'we must have a bonfire' and Lord Carrington gave 1,000 faggots and other employers in the town provided many loads of brushwood and shavings. 'The bonfire was lighted at five minutes to ten by the Mayor and soon there was a magnificent blaze, lighting up the hill and the Park and reflecting on the buildings of the town in the valley below. Thousands of people assembled on Keep Hill, in the Rye and London Road, and strains of the National Anthem were heard as the mighty sheet of flame soared higher and higher.'

40. An annual event was the Hiring Fair, which took place in and around the Guildhall during which men and women would be hired by employers for the coming season. Each carried a sign indicating their trade, the carter or nagmen would wear a piece of whipcord, the shepherds wore a tuft of wool and the cowmen put tufts of hair in their hats. The Hiring Fair took place on the Monday and Tuesday of Michaelmas, and the fair became notorious for its rough behavour. In time the townspeople managed to get it abolished in the centre of the town and moved out towards Oxford Road, but the Hiring aspect of the Fair carried on until about 1908.

41. This is the Oxford-London Coach which stopped at High Wycombe at the Falcon Hotel each day. The town was on the route of many coaches, and the High Street and Easton Street had a large number of Hotels and Public Houses to meet the demands of this very important and lucrative business. The 'Red Lion' in 1894 still had stabling for forty-five horses, while Mr. Watson, in 1877, had the best posting business in the District, with victorias, landaus and dog-carts and stabling for thirty-five horses.

42. This was the first West Wycombe to Loudwater horse bus which started in 1882, and run by Mr. Weston. He was also contractor to the Post Office and supplied horses for the local Fire Brigade. He catered for large parties, and has taken out as many as seven hundred pleasure seekers in one day. The early buses were drawn by four horses, but in time the 24 seater open-top double decker buses were pulled by two horses.

43. The horse-buses were replaced by motor buses, with the first one setting off in 1908. These were run by the Livery and Posting Company who had formerly run the horse bus. The postcard shows another parade taking place in the High Street, but also gives a good view of the south side of the road which is not often photographed.

Market House, High Wycombe.

44. The Little Market House was built to designs of Robert Adam in 1761 and is often affectionately known as the 'Pepper-pot'. It replaced the earlier building known as the 'Shambles', which had been built in 1627 on the site of the earlier 'Hog Market'. When originally planned by Adam, it was to be the 'Shambles and Butter Market', but over the years its use has changed. In 1881 the upper section was used by the Literary and Scientific Institute, at one time it was the offices of the Bucks Free Press, and now it houses the Citizen's Advice Centre.

45. Here the Little Market House and market scene circa 1880, drawn by an unknown artist and member of a drawing school based at Reading. This shows the market more on the style of the continental markets, and under the arches of the Market house hang joints of meat on iron bars. The cupola which is now on the roof has been added since this drawing, and the curve of a bow window on the extreme left marks the corner of the 'Unicorn' public house in Church Square.

46. An elegant engraving of the Guildhall and end of High Street, drawn and engraved in May 1864. The hanging signs of the 'Cross Keys' and the 'Wheat Sheaf' on the right are public houses long since gone, and the hanging sign on the left was that of 'The Falcon' next to the Guildhall.

47. The Guildhall itself has only used that name since the new Town Hall was built in Queen Victoria Road in 1904, as formerly it was the 'Great Market House' and later simply the 'Town Hall'. The present building was designed by Henry Keen and opened in 1757, it is possibly the third or fourth Guildhall the town has built, with the early ones on a site in the area bordered by White Hart Street, Church Street and Queen Square. The structure has been renovated over the years, and was strengthened and redecorated in its original style in 1982/1983.

48. Every year in May, the Guildhall is the scene of the Mayormaking Ceremony, and on that day the custom of 'Weighing in' takes place. This practice dates back to the eighteenth century, and the Mayor and the Charter Trustees and Officials are weighted on the special scales shown overleaf. Their weights are compared with the previous year, and if they have gained weight, they are booed, but if they are the same or have lost weight, they are cheered.

49. The Guildhall was also the venue for the representatives of the furniture industry in the town, when Prince Edward, later to become Edward VII, visited the town on his way to see Benjamin Disraeli at Hughenden in 1880. This chair arch was built from over three hundred chairs, and was topped by the enormous Mayor's Chair brought especially from the Council Chamber for the event. Many arches have been erected in parts of the town over the years, but this one has always been regarded as the major triumph on the part of the Furniture Industry.

50. Here are the 'Bodgers' at work in the beechwoods, having set up the temporary thatched shelter in which they turn the chair-legs and stretchers on the pole-lathe. Outside two other workers prepare the rough 'billets' or chair-legs ready for the turner to finish them ready for the factories in High Wycombe. This postcard was photographed circa 1905 and the craft carried on into the 1930's until mechanisation overtook the hand-craft worker and the factories won the day.

51. With the introduction of steam the large trees were sawn into planks in the 1860's by firms such as Plumridge's who managed with what was then modern machinery and methods, to clear the bottleneck in the furniture industry, that of preparing the timber for the factory workers at the bench. Much of the timber used in the woods by the Bodgers was unseasoned, but in time as the local supplies dried up, Wycombe furniture firms were going abroad for timbers and introduced sophisticated seasoning and kilning chambers to prepare the wood correctly.

52. The sight of the cattle strolling up the High after having been turned off the Rye by the Hayward would not be possible today with the heavy traffic which still uses the old A40 through the town. The cows wended their way through the back alleys until they arrived at their home dairy or stable at milking time. One of the more terrifying nightmares was the possibility of meeting one of these lumbering animals as one walked through the narrow alleyways between the houses in the older parts of Newlands and Bellfield.

53. The cattle market took place on the paved area behind the Guildhall in Paul's Lane, an area partly taken up now by the public conveniences. The wicker fences were set up as partitions and the cattle brought into the town for sale by auction. On one occasion in 1824, a woman was brought to the cattle market by her husband, and sold to a blacksmith for 10s. The Collector of Toll demanded, and received from the purchaser the customary ld paid on sold live stock.

54. This fine beast was brought to the market behind the Guildhall from Barmoor Farm which was on what is now Booker Airfield, in the First World War, and the farmer to the right is holding a bundle of flax which had just grown in the neighbourhood.

55. The Guildhall leads into Paul's Row, which may well take its name from the Poull Family, who lived and owned property in High Wycombe in mediaeval times. The inn plus the buildings around it have been demolished to make way for the side of the Octagon which contains Mothercare and the new Beefburger Bar.

56. The Bridge led to St. Mary Street and crossed the River Wye. This section of the Wye is now channelled beneath the road, and the Royal British Legion Head Quarters have been built next to it. There are early references in deeds to 'Benethebrugg' and this appears to refer to properties 'beneath the Bridge' i.e. beyond the bridge in St. Mary Street.

57. This section of St. Mary Street has completely gone, and has been replaced by the overhead road known as 'Abbey Way' and the College grounds. In the distance can be seen the brick building which is the last property remaining on that side of the road, now the Doctor's Surgery.

58. St. Mary Street opened out into Marlow Hill, and in this postcard the entrance gates to the Wycombe Abbey can be seen with the coronets on top of the light globes. Next to these gates was the 'Little Red Lion', further down on the same side was the 'Black Horse', and opposite was the 'Horse and Jockey' and the 'Admiral Napier'. The flooding of the road was not, even in the 1940's, an unusual sight. In St. Mary Street were several furniture factories, and at one time Hannah Ball's Wesleyan Chapel was here.

59. From the Guildhall you could see down White Hart Street, formerly called 'Hog Lane' to Queen's Square, and in the end of this picture is the building which housed Aldridges, now the fashion shop 'Country Fashions'. White Hart Street has probably had less change than most of High Wycombe's central streets, and it originally formed one side of the market area in mediaeval times.

60. The Christmas display of poultry outside Aldridges in White Hart Street always drew many spectators during the festive season. Turkeys, chicken and game hung all over the building, almost completely covering the walls. This building stood on the site of the present 'Country Fashions', on the corner of Queens Square, White Hart Street and Bull Lane. The photograph was taken in December 1931.

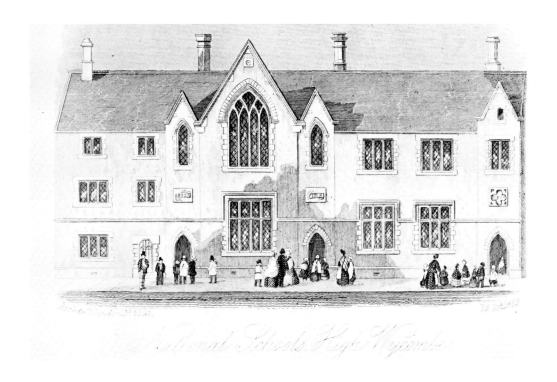

61. The National Schools, engraved here in 1863, were still standing in the 1940's and were incorporated into Murray's when their major rebuilding took place. This stood next to the White Hart Methodist Chapel, and was eventually converted into Nutt's Auction Rooms.

62. Following the road further took the visitor into Newlands, and this photograph re-creates the cobbled lanes which have be replaced by the Bus Garage and the road between Tesco's and the multi-story car park leading down the 'Gate' public house. In the distance can be seen the roof of the Methodist Chapel in White Hart Street. These houses were amongst a large number built as the town was growing in the 1840's and 1850's, and they housed many of the families working in the chair factories.

63. Back to the Guildhall, the ancient building of Chequers stands on the corner of Church Street and houses the draper's business of John R. Dring. This had been an inn in the past, and more recently was pulled down and rebuilt as a replica to retain the visual look of the corner.

64. The 'Black Boy' inn, owned by Wheeler's Brewery, catches the eye on turning the corner into Church Street. This was demolished in the 1930's in a road widening scheme, and its licence transfered to the 'Black Boy' at Terriers. Its crooked chimney was an attractive feature, and it also was at the head of a row of Tudor type cottages which extended along the side of the churchward.

65. Noyes Lane was the narrow lane, with its overhanging upper storeys, which ran from the Cornmarket entrance in Church Square, along to the 'Black Boy' in Church Street. It was demolished in the road-widening scheme of the 1930's and High Wycombe lost an attractive back lane which adjoined the church.

66. The Watch House in the Churchyard was a Tudor style building, just inside the iron gates which still separate Church Square from the churchyard proper. The Watch House was at the end of the row of cottages fronting on the Noyes Lane, and like them, disappeared in the road widening of the 1930's. It was originally the house in which the army was billeted in times of trouble, and the seventeenth century lease included this condition among its clauses.

67. The Parish Church of All Saints, as engraved about 1864. This shows the South Porch, and gives us a picture of this side of the Church before its decoration was considerable increased in the Restoration of Oldrid Scott between 1887 to 1889. The Tower was originally positioned in the centre of the Church, at the point where the Nave and Chancel join, but was demolished in 1520 and rebuilt in its present position at the west end of the nave in the 1530's.

68. The interior of All Saints was somewhat crowded in the early nineteenth century, as it had box pews until they were cut down in 1865, and a very large and ornate two storey wooden pew belonging to Wycombe Abbey in the Chancel Arch, until that also was removed to the Abbey in 1858.

69. Church Street in the 1890's shows the seventeenth century buildings which stood opposite the Churchyard. The many pitched roofs give an earlier impression than the eighteenth century brickwork of High Street offers, and this row of shops would originally have been part of the market area which in earlier times stood at their back.

70. Just across the road on the corner of Priory Road and Castle Street is 'The Priory' from which the street is named. This was originally in mediaeval times the home of the Wellesbourne family, who were Members of Parliament for the Borough. Later in the late eighteenth century General Francis Jarry, who was Inspector General of Instruction of the Royal Military College in High Street, lived here, dying in 1807, also James Gomme, antiquarian, who died in 1825.

71. Castle Street also contained several eighteenth century buildings, including 'The Chantry House' which were originally connected with the church, being houses for the chantry priests before the Reformation. The street was then known as All Hallows Lane, and included the Vicarage and Vicarage Farm.

72. Priory Road about 1900, looking back into the town, with the gates of the Wesley Chapel on the extreme left of the card. An impressive funeral is taking place, possibly connected with the Carrington family, and the cortège is making its way up to the Cemetery in Priory Road.

73. Church Street leads into Queens Square, and here on the right is part of the façade of McIlroy's store (now Marks and Spencers Ltd.) and the British School, which in 1876 became the town's Library, until it was moved to Queen Victoria Road in 1932.

74. Queens Square looking into Church Street, with the Memorial Cross in the Church-yard in the distance. Little seems to have changed, with a boot and shoe shop still on the corner on the right.

75. Queen Square, looking toward the 'Hen and Chicken' with the 'Lion in the Wood' inn-sign hanging on the left of the picture. It was here that Hannah Ball lived with her brother for some years, looking after his children, when she was involved in starting her Sunday School in the town.

76. From Church Square into Oxford Street, and on the right opens the wide area of Frogmoor. The shop on the corner facing us is now Hearns, the shoe shop.

77. Frogmore fountain about 1890, showing the west side of the square looking down to the 'Bell Inn'. The fountain itself has gone, demolished during the early years of the war, with the metal going, as did all railings and gates in the town, to the War Effort.

FROGMOOR GARDENS, HIGH WYCOMBE.

78. Frogmoor Fountain some years later, with the trees grown into fine specimens. This shows the east side of the square with the small cottage like building at the point of the Frogmore paved area, where the fire engine was kept prior to the new Fire Station being built in Priory Road in 1901.

79. At the end of Frogmoor was the Salvation Army Hall which had formerly been the Methodist Chapel until the new one was built in White Hart Street in 1875. The Salvation Army moved into the old chapel in 1882, and moved to their present building on the other side of Frogmore 1909.

80. The distinctive building near the bridge in Frogmore is often called the 'Intimate Theatre', but it started its life as the Science and Art School in 1893 at a cost of £2,200. When the old Grammar School in Easton Street became vacant in 1915, most of the departments of this school moved there, although the site was retained for a further ten years. In 1929 it was converted into a swimming pool, and then in 1946 it became the town's repertory theatre. During the 1960's and 1970's it remained unused, becoming more and more in a state of disrepair, until in 1983 it has been sold to Crest Estates Ltd., to be developed for office accommodation.

81. Frogmoor, even today, is the 'Hyde Park' corner of the town, with demonstrations, fringe group speakers or religious bodies attracting the attention of the passersby. Here the advertisers took over in the 1920's and 'Salmon Teas' rose in the air to the delight of the large audience below.

82. Frogmoor in the 1920's shows the crowded effect that the increase of business and traffic had on the town, with pseudo-Tudor buildings on the left and the right dominating what was formerly a pleasant wide square.

83. Oxford Street runs along the side of Frogmoor, and leads with its shops into Oxford Road out to the west side of High Wycombe. The Electroscope Theatre with its plaster decoration is on the left, this became the 'Rex' in the 1930's.

84. Oxford Street looking back to the 'Hen and Chickens' in Queen Square gives an entirely different scene than at present. Hull Loosley and Pierce are on the right, next to the opening which is Bowdery's Lane. All this has gone to make way for the Oxford Road Island.

85. Oxford Road is seen as a quiet street with substantial houses and the River Wye running between the houses and railings alongside the pavement.

Oxford Rd High Wycombe

86. Oxford Road looking west shows the river to advantage, each group of houses with their own footbridge, and the road winding into the distance, past the Carrington Arms.

87. Oxford Road at the Oxford Street end had the shops continuing along the north side of the road with the terraces fronting on the river standing on what is now the Oxford Road open car park, and the river culverted under the road.

88. Doel's Stores were No. 76 Oxford Road, next to Carrington Cottages. It was listed as a cycle agent, but obviously from the picture sold mangles, iron bedstead, prams and many other things as well.

89. Bridge Street, with Zion Strict Baptist Church on the corner, and the 'Royal Oak' public house only a few yards down the road. Further down were the Bridge Street Saw Mills and the 'Old Victoria' public house nearer Desborough Road on the same side.

Desborough Road, High Wycombe

90. Desborough Road was formerly known as Watery Lane, and before that as St. John's Lane was the main road out of High Wycombe to West Wycombe before Sir Francis Dashwood built the West Wycombe Road in the eighteenth century. It has always been a separate shopping centre to that of the town and created its own community.

91. St. John's Church, Desborough was designed by W.D. Caroe and consecrated in 1903, this replaced an earlier iron building erected 1882/1883, both of which appear to be shown on this postcard. The present building, consisting of nave and chancel, has recently celebrated its centenary.

WEST WYCOMBE. CHAPEL LANE BRIDGE.

92. Along the West Wycombe Road, the turning to Chapel Lane seems inconspicious, but it led at one time to what was a separate small village, and the lane led over a narrow bridge with its flint constructed follies to Sands.

93. Sands in the 1920's was still in the country, with the village primary school in the centre of the picture. Gradually the housing and since the Second World War the industrial estates have grown up to make it almost an indistinguishable part of High Wycombe.

94. Bellfield lies at the end of the hillside overlooking the town from the west, and this print of the 1860's shows it nestled in the valley surrounded by hills and trees.

BIRDSEYE VIEW OF HIGH WYCOMBE.

95. Birdseye view of High Wycombe from Bellfield in the 1890's from almost the same position has the factories playing a more prominent part in the landscape. The Church still stands clearly above the other buildings, and the new Wesleyan Methodist Chapel in Priory Avenue, opened in 1875, is clear on the right.

96. View of High Wycombe about 1890 with the camera moving west to show up the building taking place on this side of the town. The White Hart Street Methodist Church opened in 1875 and its roof stands out above the other houses, while next to it is the National School established in 1855.

97. Crendon Street opened off the High Street and led to Amersham. Until the widening scheme of the 1930's it was extremely narrow. Weller's public house the 'White Horse' was at one end of the lane, nearest to High Street with the 'White Lion' at the other, nearer the Railway Station.

98. Crendon Street 1922 has the spire of Christchurch on the righthand side. This Church was built to designs of Arthur Vernon for the breakaway parish of Christchurch in 1889.

99. The Railway Yard at the top of Crendon Street with Castle Street stretching into the distance. The horse-buses of L. Weston stand to the right of the gateway, with the Temperance Hotel opposite. Castle Street was originally only a foot path from the farm through to Crendon Street, but in the late nineteenth century it was made up, and then Corporation Street opened up, both to give easier access to the Railway Station for the west side of the town.

100. Amersham Hill was being built up in the 1890's onwards, chiefly with large houses built for or purchased by the prosperous chair manufacturers. These have since changed hands, and in some cases have been converted to commercial use, others have been demolished to make room for blocks of flats, but higher up the hill, the Godstowe School has purchased a number to extend the limits of their accommodation.

101. Looking back down Amersham Hill, the valley and the open grounds of Wycombe Abbey can be seen. The Hill runs alongside the 'Old British Way' which was the original footpath up to Terriers and on to Hazlemere. This still remains, but more commonly called Cemetary Path, and it runs behind Ridgeway and Brands Hill Avenue, continuing behind Wellesbourne School.

102. Terriers was a hamlet or group of cottages, clustered at the top of Amersham Hill continuing up to the Tollgate House which stood on the site of Drew's the Baker next to Terriers First School. The Royal Grammar School was moved to the brow of the hill in 1915 and the building of the Green Street, Tower Street and Great Kingshill houses has been followed by extensive private housing in adjacent streets, linking Terriers to the Amersham Hill.

103. Terriers Tollgate House was one of three tollgates in the High Wycombe area, and stood on the edge of the town on the toll road from Hatfield to the Bath Road (the A4). The story goes that this road was built to enable the family at Hatfield House to more easily visit Bath and partake of the Bath waters. This Tollhouse was demolished in recent times and the two shops, the Baker shop and Butcher shop adjacent to the School, built on its site. The lane to the left leads to Great Kingshill, while that to right leads to Totteridge and Hatters Lane.

104. The top of Totteridge Lane about 1910. This was farmland on the outskirts of Terriers. The Lane itself turned at the Catholic Church to come back into town, while its present extension, called Hatters Lane, was opened up in the early years of the twentieth century, to give vehicular access to the London Road.

105. Bowerdean Farm in 1905 lies nestled in the valley, surrounded by the field it ploughed, seeded and harvested to bring grain into the mills of High Wycombe. This whole aspect of country life has changed, so too the landscape, as the 'Morning Star' has replaced the Farm, and the whole countryside has been developed with housing in all directions. Bowerdean itself was probably at one time church land, belonging to the Bower Chapel in the Church of All Saints, for Castle Hill, which is adjacent to the Church, was once known as Bower Hayes.

106. The railway arrived at High Wycombe as a branch line from Maidenhead, and opened for traffic 1st August 1854, and the line was extended to Thame in August 1862 and in 1864 it was further extended to Oxford. The mail coach from London was discontinued in 1842 and letters came by cart from Oxford. This postcard shows the high embankment necessary to carry the railway line across the bottom of the Wye Valley, and the viaduct at Frogmore with its single track.

107. The Railway was converted to standard gauge in 1867, and in 1904 a large force of men shifted the down line near the platform of the new stations as the doubling of the line became necessary. Additional work included the widening of the culvert which ran alongside Priory Avenue, shown here, and the mammoth task of building a second viaduct at the end of Frogmore to carry the second line. In 1906 a new direct railway line was opened, which led to Marylebone.

108. The Cemetery in Priory Road was filling up by the 1890's, so were the southern hills of the valley, with roads and houses extending from Desborough Road along towards Sands, and up into Oakridge and later into Cressex and Booker. The 1930's was the end of the close community life of High Wycombe, and the 1950's and 1960's took their toll on the buildings in the centre of the town itself, changing, in the view of many, the actual nature of the town itself.